This book belongs to

____

____

____

Stay Home!

Create a scavenger hunt!

This can be using objects, phones, inside, or in the yard.

Could even use memories as scavenger hunt ideas.

Be creative!

Her Reaction

____

____

____

____

____

____

____

His Reaction

____

____

____

____

____

____

____

Do This Again Sometime?

Yes ☐   No ☐

Go Out!

Enjoy a Spa Day

Book a day at a spa and have fun getting pampered for the day!

Her Reaction

____
____
____
____
____
____
____

His Reaction

____
____
____
____
____
____
____

Do This Again Sometime?

Yes [ ]   No [ ]

Tipsy!

Go to a paint and sip.

It's so much fun to create a painting, have some wine together, and meet other people.

These are also available online!

Her Reaction

His Reaction

Do This Again Sometime?

Yes ☐　　No ☐

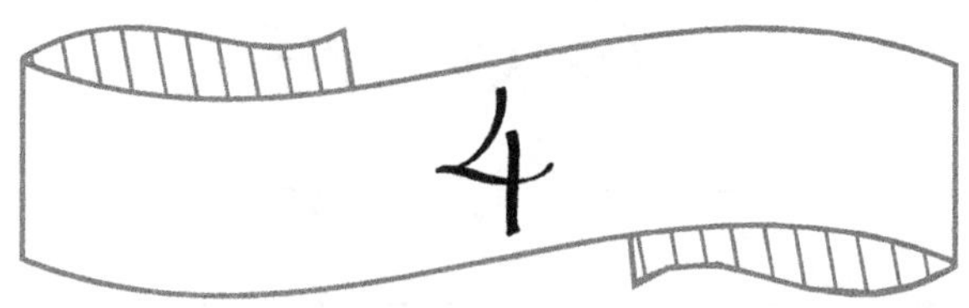

Camping!

Go camping together and enjoy the outdoors.

If you can, try to be nude a bit outdoors, or even some outdoor sex.

Her Reaction

____

____

____

____

____

____

His Reaction

____

____

____

____

____

____

Do This Again Sometime?

Yes [ ]   No [ ]

Karaoke

Go to a local bar and sing karaoke together!

Dress up sexy and sing a few duet songs together.

Her Reaction

His Reaction

Do This Again Sometime?

Yes ☐   No ☐

Stay In!

Play board games together. Monopoly, Twister, or any other classics.

If desired, create fun "strip" elements to get the clothes off easily.

Her Reaction

His Reaction

Do This Again Sometime?

Yes   No

Go Out!

Play Mini Golf

Just have fun acting like kids for the night.

Her Reaction

His Reaction

Do This Again Sometime?

Yes   No

Dinner

Go out to a new
Restaurant that you've
never been to.

Make sure to dress up
sexy for each other.

Her Reaction

His Reaction

Do This Again Sometime?

Yes ☐   No ☐

Get Outdoors!

Go out on a hike at nearby hiking trail.

Use "All Trails" app to find a nearby trail.

Bonus points for any sexual fun in the woods!

Her Reaction

____

____

____

____

____

____

His Reaction

____

____

____

____

____

____

Do This Again Sometime?

Yes ☐   No ☐

Go Shopping!

Go shopping together for either a common interest or something sexy.

Bonus points: Go shopping for lingerie or sex toys together.

Her Reaction

His Reaction

Do This Again Sometime?

Yes ☐   No ☐

Stay In!

Have an evening of "No Clothes Allowed"

Everything you do for the evening, will be in the nude.

No clothes all night long!

Her Reaction

His Reaction

Do This Again Sometime?

Yes [ ]   No [ ]

Lights, Camera, Action!

Have a photo shoot!

Stay in and take pictures of each other. This could be in various places in the house, or sexy pics in the bedroom!

Spice it up!

Her Reaction

____

____

____

____

____

____

His Reaction

____

____

____

____

____

____

____

Do This Again Sometime?

Yes ☐   No ☐

Learn Something!

Learn a new hobby or skill together.

Get a new course online to learn together, or on Youtube.

Her Reaction

His Reaction

Do This Again Sometime?

Yes [ ]   No [ ]

Picnic Time!

This could be at a nearby park, lake, beach, or even in your backyard.

Bonus points for dressing sexy and being naughty.

Her Reaction

____

____

____

____

____

____

____

His Reaction

____

____

____

____

____

____

____

Do This Again Sometime?

Yes ☐   No ☐

Time To Laugh!

Go to a local comedy club for dinner and a comedy show.

Bonus points for being the heckler at the show.

Her Reaction

____

____

____

____

____

____

____

His Reaction

____

____

____

____

____

____

____

Do This Again Sometime?

Yes ☐   No ☐

Volunteer Together

There must be something you both care about.

This makes a perfect opportunity to volunteer together helping this cause.

Her Reaction

____

____

____

____

____

____

His Reaction

____

____

____

____

____

____

Do This Again Sometime?

Yes ☐   No ☐

Bake Together!

Who doesn't like brownies or cookies?

Stay in and bake together, enjoying some sweets and each other's company.

Bonus points for baking together in sexy lingerie/clothing.

Her Reaction

____

____

____

____

____

____

____

His Reaction

____

____

____

____

____

____

____

Do This Again Sometime?

Yes ☐   No ☐

Some Drinks

Go out to a local brewery or winery for some tasting and drinking fun.

Her Reaction

____

____

____

____

____

____

____

His Reaction

____

____

____

____

____

____

____

Do This Again Sometime?

Yes [ ]   No [ ]

Scenic Drive

Take a scenic drive together in the nearby area.

You may discover new places you didn't realize were around you.

Bonus points for fooling around in the car!

Her Reaction

____

____

____

____

____

____

____

His Reaction

____

____

____

____

____

____

____

Do This Again Sometime?

Yes ☐   No ☐

20 Questions

Stay in and ask each other 20 questions.

These could be about life, future goals, sex, fantasies, or mix it all up!

Her Reaction

____

____

____

____

____

____

____

His Reaction

____

____

____

____

____

____

____

Do This Again Sometime?

Yes ☐   No ☐

Rent A Boat

Having some fun outside together is great for relationships.

Rent jetski's, boat, or any other outdoor fun mobiles.

Her Reaction

____

____

____

____

____

____

____

His Reaction

____

____

____

____

____

____

Do This Again Sometime?

Yes ☐   No ☐

Adult Flix

Stay in and watch some adult films together.

Lay in bed or couch nude together. No touching for the first 20 mins!

Her Reaction

____

____

____

____

____

____

____

His Reaction

____

____

____

____

____

____

____

Do This Again Sometime?

Yes ☐   No ☐

Musuem/Aquarim/Zoo

Visiting local attractions together are fun.

Look for a local musuem or similar attraction to visit together.

Her Reaction

____

____

____

____

____

____

His Reaction

____

____

____

____

____

____

Do This Again Sometime?

Yes ☐   No ☐

Sex Club

Visit a local Sex or Swingers Club.

Don't worry, you don't need to play with other people to have fun.

Her Reaction

His Reaction

Do This Again Sometime?

Yes   ☐   No   ☐

Farmers Market

Visit a local Farmer's Market or similar place.

It's fun to go vegetable and flower shopping.

Her Reaction

____

____

____

____

____

____

____

His Reaction

____

____

____

____

____

____

____

Do This Again Sometime?

Yes ☐   No ☐

Carnival Fun

Go to a local festival, carnival, or even amusement park.

Act like kids all night having fun on rides and games.

Can also stay in and create your own carnival!

Her Reaction

____

His Reaction

____

Do This Again Sometime?

Yes [ ]   No [ ]

Memories

Look at old pictures together and reminsce of old times.

Wedding, honeymoon, vacations, birthdays, and more.

Her Reaction

____

____

____

____

____

____

____

____

His Reaction

____

____

____

____

____

____

____

____

Do This Again Sometime?

Yes ☐　　　No ☐

Crafts Fun

Stay in and have a craft night. Search online for easy crafts that you can both create together.

Her Reaction

____

____

____

____

____

____

____

His Reaction

____

____

____

____

____

____

____

Do This Again Sometime?

Yes ☐   No ☐

Dancing!

Take local dance lessons together learning a new type of dancing.

If not available, stay in and learn by searching Youtube.

Her Reaction

His Reaction

Do This Again Sometime?

Yes ☐   No ☐

Sex!

Now that we are at the end. Let's have some great sex trying at least 3 new sex positions you haven't done ever, or in a long time.

In the next 24 hours, aim to have sex 3 times. This will get the ball rolling for increased sexual intimacy.

Her Reaction

____

____

____

____

____

____

____

His Reaction

____

____

____

____

____

____

____

Do This Again Sometime?

Yes ☐   No ☐